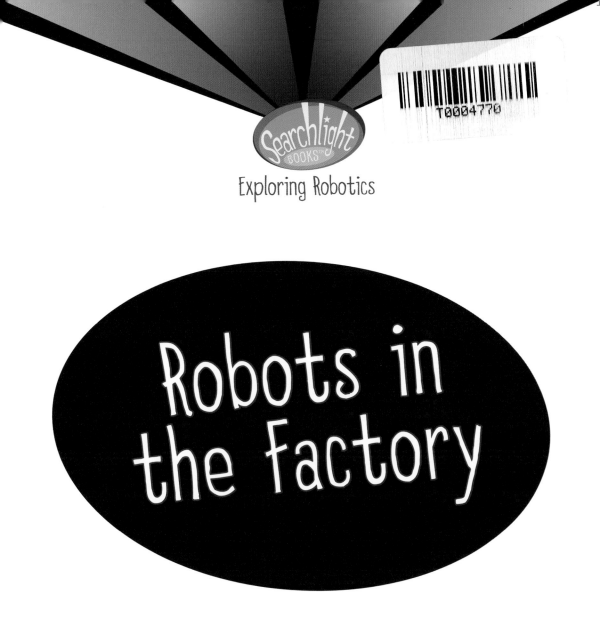

Searchlight
BOOKS™

Exploring Robotics

Robots in the Factory

Lisa Idzikowski

Lerner Publications ◆ Minneapolis

for my family

Lerner Publications Company
An imprint of Lerner Publishing Group, Inc.
241 First Avenue North
Minneapolis, MN 55401 USA

For reading levels and more information, look up this title at www.lernerbooks.com.

Main body text set in Adrianna Regular.
Typeface provided by Chank.

Library of Congress Cataloging-in-Publication Data

Names: Idzikowski, Lisa, author.
Title: Robots in the factory / Lisa Idzikowski.
Description: Minneapolis : Lerner Publications, [2024] | Series: Searchlight books. Exploring robotics | Includes bibliographical references and index. | Audience: Ages 8–11 | Audience: Grades 4–6 | Summary: "From lifting heavy objects to assembling products, robots do many different jobs in factories. Explore the past, present, and future of factory robots, including how they work and how their design might change next"— Provided by publisher.
Identifiers: LCCN 2022037379 (print) | LCCN 2022037380 (ebook) | ISBN 9781728476773 (library binding) | ISBN 9798765600153 (ebook)
Subjects: LCSH: Robots—Juvenile literature. | Robotics—Social aspects—Juvenile literature.
Classification: LCC TJ211.2 .I3925 2024 (print) | LCC TJ211.2 (ebook) | DDC 629.8/92—dc23/eng/20220902

LC record available at https://lccn.loc.gov/2022037379
LC ebook record available at https://lccn.loc.gov/2022037380

Manufactured in the United States of America
1-52258-50698-10/17/2022

Table of Contents

Chapter 1

ROBOTS MAKE IT

Press the dough into a circle. Spread tomato sauce all over. Sprinkle with cheese and other toppings. Place in an oven to cook. Many people enjoy making and eating pizza. But would pizza be just as delicious if a robot made it? In some factory kitchens, robots are doing just that.

There are many kinds of factories. Some make foods such as pizza or ice cream that are frozen and sold in stores. Other factories put together products such as cars, cell phones, or computers. Many people work in factories. They use special technology such as robots to do their jobs.

A robotic arm moving a pizza to a box

Factory workers sometimes have to work with dangerous tools or materials.

Safer Work

Jobs in factories can be challenging. Some jobs require workers to lift heavy objects or use dangerous chemicals or burning-hot materials. Other tasks must be repeated without a break. This type of work can cause people to lose their focus. Dangerous materials and tiring work can lead to accidents and mistakes. People could get hurt. Is there a way to keep people safe doing dangerous or tiring factory jobs?

One way is to put robots to work instead. Factory robots are robots used in factories and warehouses. They can take on unsafe work to help keep human workers safe.

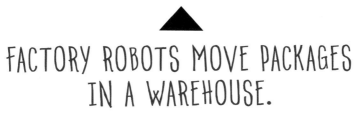

FACTORY ROBOTS MOVE PACKAGES IN A WAREHOUSE.

Parts of a Factory Robot

One of the most common types of factory robots are robotic arms. The armlike machines can twist, turn, and grab things. These machines have a controller. It is like a brain. Programs inside their controller, along with sensors and vision systems, help guide the robot's actions. For example, some robotic arms have sensors that tell them if they bump into something. Actuators get the arms moving.

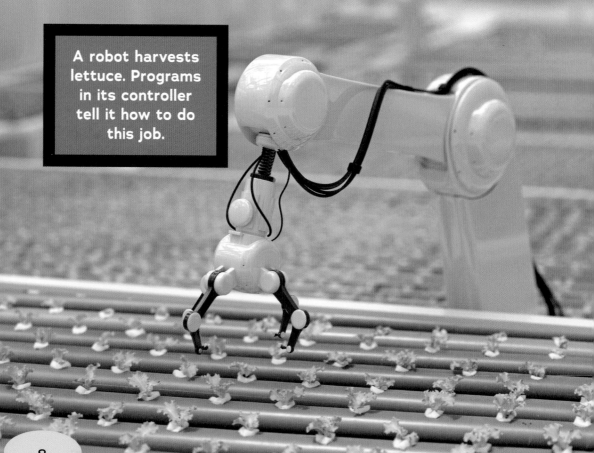

A robot harvests lettuce. Programs in its controller tell it how to do this job.

SOME END EFFECTORS ARE USED TO GRIP AND GRAB OBJECTS.

▼

An important part of a factory robotic arm is its end effector. This tool on a robot acts like a hand. The tool looks different and does different things depending on the job the robot was built for. Some factory robots have grippers to pick up objects. They might pick up boxes or heavy car parts and move them around. Others are experts at painting. The Kawasaki KJ264 has a paint sprayer and can paint cars. Many products are made in factories with the help of robots. Whether in a car factory, a candy bar factory, or somewhere else, robots get factory jobs done quickly.

The Kawasaki MX500 robot can lift heavy objects such as motorcycles.

Chapter 2

INVENTING A ROBOT

In the early 1900s, the Ford Model T was one of the first cars to be mass-produced. That's when large amounts of something are made quickly, often with the help of machines. Workers put the cars together in assembly lines. Assembly lines reduce the time it takes to put products together. Assembly lines were popular and used in many kinds of factories. But was there a way to make the process even easier?

A Ford Model T assembly line in 1915. Assembly lines are still popular in factories.

During the Industrial Revolution (1760–1840), people started using more machines to help them build things more easily. Technology improved. In the mid-1900s, engineers, or people who build machines and technology, created robots that could work in factories.

In 1954, American inventor George Devol filed for a patent for the first factory robot. It was a robotic arm. In 1956, Devol teamed up with Joseph F. Engelberger, an American engineer who believed the robot could work. They thought it could move parts in a factory. The men worked on the robot for over two years. By 1959, they made a working model of their machine, the Unimate #001. The first factory robot was ready to work.

The company Unimation went on to make many more robots such as this modern one.

Key Figure

Joseph F. Engelberger was an American scientist and engineer. He received many engineering awards and is known around the world as the Father of Robotics. Engelberger was committed to helping make jobs easier with robots. Over twenty years after helping develop Unimate #001, he formed a new company that created service robots for hospitals and nursing homes.

A 1980 Unimation robot types on a keyboard.

Devol and Engelberger showed Unimate #001 to the directors of factories and explained how the machine could help keep workers safe. The new robot could do many jobs, especially the dangerous ones. It could handle heavy, hot objects that workers struggled to move and work with safely. General Motors, one of the largest carmakers, put the Unimate #001 model into their car factory in Trenton, New Jersey, in 1959. By 1961, the Unimate 1900 series became the first mass-produced robotic arm for factories.

A robot pouring a cup of tea in the United Kingdom in the 1960s

Becoming Popular

Robotics technology continued to improve in the United States and elsewhere. By the late 1960s, the technology had spread to Japan and many European countries such as Sweden and Norway. One factory in Norway even began using robots to paint wheelbarrows.

Engineers and other workers who focus on robotics continue to develop new robot technology. In the beginning, these machines were mainly at car factories. But robots have become more common in all types of factories.

MANY CAR FACTORIES USE ROBOTS TO BUILD, PAINT, AND MOVE CARS.

Chapter 3

FACTORIES AND FULFILLMENT CENTERS

Imagine working in a candy factory all day. Would your fingers get tired from putting candy pieces into packages? Meet Lucy and Ethel. They never get tired of placing candy into trays. They certainly don't get sticky fingers! These two machines are IRB 340 FlexPicker robots. They work in a factory for the Wolfgang Candy Company in York, Pennsylvania. Many robots like Lucy and Ethel are hard at work in factories worldwide.

Lucy and Ethel are FlexPickers like this one and were named after 1950s television characters.

Many Robotic Arms

Since Unimate #001 arrived on the factory floor in 1956, robots have been a key part of automation in car factories. The Tesla car factory in Fremont, California, has about seven hundred robots. Most of them are robotic arms made by the KUKA or FANUC robot companies and work from inside caged areas. Ten of the largest, most powerful of them are named after comic book characters. Vulcan and Havok work together and lift cars onto a rail where they are put together. Then Xavier safely moves cars from an electric rail down to the floor. Beast, Iceman, and Wolverine lift heavy items. They're so powerful that some of them can lift entire cars!

Cars being assembled in a Tesla factory

A robot putting together batteries

Not all robotic arms are meant to handle such heavy loads. Stäubli, a Swiss company, makes its HE robots for food factories. Big Drum Engineering uses the Stäubli TX90 HE as part of a machine called the Robot Filler. It fills large tubs of ice cream. Another robotic arm, the TX200L HE, helps a cheesemaking company in Germany. With its special gripper that looks like the prongs of a forklift, this robot moves 176-pound (80 kg) wheels of cheese around the factory to shelves, racks, and more.

Look at It Move!

Some robots move around factories without help from people. Autonomous mobile robots get around by using machine vision. This technology lets the machine see where it can go without running into other objects and people.

A robot moving through a warehouse by itself

ar
348205

In 2021, Amazon was testing four robots built to help workers. One was Ernie, which lifts bins from shelves and uses a robotic arm to deliver them to workers. Three were autonomous mobile robots. The robot Bert carries things around a fulfillment center, a warehouse where orders are packed and shipped to customers.

AMAZON USES MANY ROBOTS SUCH AS THIS ROBOTIC ARM THAT SORTS AND STACKS BINS.

Workers can call Bert to carry objects such as packages for them. This saves them time and energy. Two other robots called Scooter and Kermit move carts filled with plastic bins or packages around the center. All four robots were being tested to help Amazon workers get orders filled faster for delivery.

Having robots help move things like bins lets human workers focus on other tasks.

Chapter 4

WHAT'S NEXT?

Robots have helped factories in many ways. Many people believe that robots will only become more common, especially in factories. But that's not the only likely change for factory robots. Experts think automation can still improve by making smaller, safer, or cheaper robots.

Collaborative Robots

Cobots, or collaborative robots, are newer types of robots that can work safely with people near them. Compared to other factory robots, cobots are smaller and lighter weight, and some are made of softer materials. Cobots have sensors that make them stop if they touch a person. Because cobots are smaller than big robotic arms like Unimation arms, they can fit in tighter spaces. They can be set up quickly and are easier to program and use. Cobots are also much cheaper than bigger robots.

A worker arranging flowers with a cobot

A worker programs a robot. Programs can make robots pack lunches, build objects, and more.

One example of a cobot is the UR5e. Made in Denmark, it weighs 45 pounds (20 kg) and can lift up to 11 pounds (5 kg). Workers can teach this robot what to do by moving its arms. Then the robot can copy the motion. Workers can also use a tablet computer to guide it. The UR5e is especially good for picking things up and setting them down. One time, a group of these machines spent the day packing food for kids. A UR5e picked up to six packages of food and snacks and placed them into bags. Then another UR5e sealed the bag and set it aside to be grabbed by a third robot.

Working with Robots

As technology improves, more robots will be working in factories and elsewhere. People will be needed to design, build, and program new robots. Maybe you'll design a new type of robotic arm! Robots will continue to help make factories safer and faster.

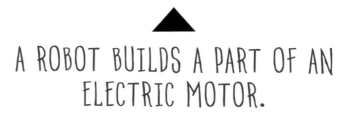

A ROBOT BUILDS A PART OF AN ELECTRIC MOTOR.

STEM Spotlight

Software is the programs and information that tells a computer such as a robot's controller what to do. People called robotics software engineers write code, or computer instructions, for software that tells a robot how, when, or if to move or act. Software can tell a robot how to put a product together, lift and move something around, paint an object, and more.

Glossary

actuator: a tool for moving or controlling something

automation: a method of making a machine, process, or system work without direct control by a person

autonomous: able to act on its own

collaborative: something or someone that works with others

controller: the computer in a robot that controls its actions and functions

end effector: a handlike tool connected to the end of a robotic arm

patent: a document that excludes others from making or selling an invention for a certain number of years

robotics: technology dealing with robots in automation

sensor: a device that detects information and sends it to the robotic controller

Learn More

Girls Into Coding
    https://www.girlsintocoding.com

Hamilton, S. L. *Industrial Robots*. Minneapolis: Abdo, 2019.

Miller, Derek. *The STEM of Robots*. New York: Cavendish Square, 2021.

National Geographic: What Is a Robot?
    https://education.nationalgeographic.org/resource/what-robot

Robot Facts for Kids
    https://kids.kiddle.co/Robot

Sonneborn, Liz. *Robots at Home*. Minneapolis: Lerner Publications, 2024.

Index

Photo Acknowledgments

Image credits:BERTRAND GUAY/Getty Images, p. 5; Andy Sacks/Getty Images, p. 6; imaginima/Getty Images, p. 7; andresr/Getty Images, p.8; Yuichiro Chino/Getty Images, p. 9; Koichi Kamoshida/Stringer, p. 10; National Motor Museum/Heritage Images/Getty Images, p. 12; SSPL/Getty Images, p. 13; John Nobley/Fairfax Media/Getty Images, p. 14; WS Collection/Alamy Stock Photo, p. 15; Gamma-Keystone/Getty Images, p. 16; Robert Gilhooly/Bloomberg/Getty Images, p. 17; REUTERS/Thomas Peter/Alamy Stock Photo, p. 19; Patrick Pleul/picture alliance/Getty Images, p. 20; FOTO/Future Publishing/Getty Images, p. 21; Watchara Phomicinda/MediaNews Group/The Press-Enterprise/Getty Images, pp. 22, 23; Ina Fassbender/picture alliance/Getty Images, p. 24; The Asahi Shimbun/Getty Images, p. 26; CFOTO/Future Publishing/Getty Images, p. 27; JOHN MACDOUGALL/AFP/Getty Images, p. 28.

Cover: Kerem Uzel/Bloomberg/Getty Images.